P9-CEV-769

STRESS

How to Cope at
the End of Your Rope

JUNE HUNT

ROSE PUBLISHING/ASPIRE PRESS

Torrance, California

ROSE PUBLISHING/ASPIRE PRESS

CONTENTS

ear Friend,

Has unrelenting stress ever pushed you to the breaking point? Have you ever felt that if one more pressure was added to your life, you would snap? If so, you are not alone. How well I remember a time in my own life when I thought: *I can't take any more stress—I can't handle one more thing!*

I felt deeply wounded and betrayed in a relationship. Words were spoken that weren't true, and the stress it caused in my life was intense. And because our ministry—HOPE FOR THE HEART—was in its infancy, the daily "to-do" lists were filled beyond my ability to accomplish it all.

As a result, my physical body felt the impact. Though I'd go to bed late, working until past midnight (I am a confirmed night owl), I began waking up each morning at 4:00. And when I awoke, I was instantly alert—my mind racing through the endless list of tasks necessary to meet the real needs of others.

Understand, waking up before sunrise has never been my norm. (I always thought that if the Lord wanted me to see the sun rise, He would have scheduled it later in the day!) Nevertheless, these early awakenings were truly beneficial, enabling me to get even more work done. Yet several months later, the Lord showed me that my rising abnormally early had nothing to do with increased productivity. Instead, my sleep disturbance had everything to do with *stress*—specifically, the painful pressure of a broken relationship.

As difficult as the physical burden was, its *emotional* toll was even weightier. Our young, help-filled ministry—always such a joy before—began to feel like a two-ton boulder on my back. I didn't have the help I needed to answer all of the counseling letters. I didn't have the confidence to do all the research required for my teaching on so many subjects. I didn't have a way to release all the mounting pressure of ministering to so many others. This period in my life was such a blessing and a burden at the same time.

And then there was the weight of my own wrong choices. As my mind churned day after day, I couldn't rightly place full blame on the other person. My acute awareness of that fact created even more perturbing pressure. "*If only* I'd made different decisions. *If only* I'd thought a different way. *If only* I'd been a different person. *If only ... If only ...* "

By God's grace, it was at this point that I began to meditate on one of the most precious and poignant verses: "*The Lord himself goes before you and will be with you; he will never leave you nor forsake you. Do not be afraid; do not be discouraged*" (Deut. 31:8). This passage and several others, coupled with the wise counsel of friends, helped me turn a spiritual corner. Slowly, as I began surrendering my burdens to the Lord, my stress began to dissipate as quietly as it had arrived.

Since that time, I've learned that stress can have either a positive or negative impact in our lives. On the positive side, it can increase our ability to endure. On the negative side, it can cause us to break.

Mindful of these dynamics, when a blacksmith applies heat in the process of hammering out a horseshoe, he not only shapes the metal but also increases its strength. Likewise, when God places us on His holy anvil and allows us to come into contact with the heated hammer of circumstances, it is never for the purpose of harming us. Instead, under His care, He will both shape and strengthen us. Only then can we accomplish His perfect plan for our lives.

Never forget, God knows you intimately. He knows the right amount of pressure to permit into your life. Even so, your response to that stress is critical. When you surrender yourself to the perfect hands of the Master Craftsman, you then invite Him to reproduce the life of Christ in you, creating a work of art worthy of His use.

For years, the following words were attached to my bathroom mirror, reminding me of this life-changing truth:

> There is nothing—
> No circumstance, no trouble, no testing—
> That can ever touch me until, first of all,
> It has gone past God and past Christ,
> Right through to me.
> If it has come that far, it has come with great
>   purpose,
> Which I may not understand at the moment;
> But as I refuse to become panicky,
> As I lift my eyes up to Him
> And accept it as coming from the throne of God

For some great purpose of blessing to my own
heart,
No sorrow will ever disturb me,
No trial will ever disarm me,
No circumstance will cause me to fret,
For I shall rest in the joy of what my Lord is.*

You personally can "be at rest" amidst your trials if you focus, not on your trials, but on your God, who is sovereign over your trials. He knows how to use the stress in your life to bless your life!

During my own deepest times of stress, one particular Scripture has continued to comfort my heart—and I pray it will comfort you:

"We are hard pressed on every side, but not crushed; perplexed, but not in despair; persecuted, but not abandoned; struck down, but not destroyed" (2 Corinthians 4:8–9).

Yours in the Lord's hope,

June

June Hunt

---

* Alan Redpath, *Victorious Christian Living* (Old Tappan, NJ: Fleming H. Revell, 1951), 166.

STRESS
How to Cope at the End of Your Rope

Are you *stressed out* and barreling down the road to *burnout*?

Stress can be a motivator or a mean taskmaster, unceasingly pressuring you, relentlessly threatening you. You can feel like you are carrying the weight of the world on your shoulders. Yet what an extraordinary relief when you realize the truth that your burden is carried by Someone else.

Jesus invites you: *"Come to me, all you who are weary and burdened, and I will give you rest"* (Matthew 11:28). God's will for your life is not continual stress, but rather confident rest. You can be confident that in every circumstance He is at work within you. God intends that your stress send you straight into the Savior's arms.

Your Burden Bearer can shoulder it all, including the most stressful of experiences that send some spiraling downward to a halt.

Are you at the breaking point right now? Do you feel that one more pressure added to your life will break you? If you feel like you're about to break, you can lighten your load by letting Him bear your burdens! Remember, stress can be a mean taskmaster, but stress can also be a motivator.

"It matters not how great the pressure is, only where the pressure lies. As long as the pressure does not come between me and my Savior, but presses me to Him, then the greater the pressure, the greater my dependence upon Him."—Hudson Taylor [1]

> "Cast all your anxiety on him
> because he cares for you."
> (1 Peter 5:7)

The 16th president of the United States, *Abraham Lincoln*, is a man universally acknowledged to be no stranger to stress. It pulled Lincoln down to the depths of despair time and time again. Yet each time, by an act of his will he rose up, recognizing that he didn't want to leave this life without greatly contributing to it.

Among the most beloved and respected of all American presidents, his stellar accomplishments proved that great success often comes from great stress.

> "I was pushed back and about to fall,
> but the LORD helped me.
> The LORD is my strength and my defense;
> he has become my salvation."
> (Psalm 118:13–14)

DEFINITIONS

Abraham Lincoln grew up with stress as a constant companion, emotionally troubling him and eventually enveloping him.

An impoverished and tragic childhood—marked by the deaths of his mother, aunt, uncle, and beloved sister, as well as the neglect of an emotionally absent father—proved to be the stressful opening chapter to a life that would be punctuated by pain and anguish.

As an adult, *melancholy* became a common word to describe Lincoln's demeanor. He lived in a state of sadness that drew both the attention and the sympathy of those around him.

But in August 1835 another word became associated with Lincoln—*unstable*—as a painfully stressful event led to a complete emotional breakdown.[2]

His experience could be likened to that of the psalmist:

"I am worn out from my groaning.
All night long I flood my bed with weeping
and drench my couch with tears.
My eyes grow weak with sorrow."
(Psalm 6:6–7)

Anna Mayes Rutledge was a lovely young woman with big blue eyes and silky blonde hair that gently flowed across her shoulders. Anna was the apple of Abraham Lincoln's eye and the picture of health, until an epidemic swept across rural Illinois, debilitating her with what doctors then described as "bilious fever."

Lincoln had tended to the sick, built coffins, and assisted with burials. Now the health crisis became intensely personal and deeply distressing, prompting him to make repeated visits to Anna's bedside.

For months, stress had been coming at Lincoln from seemingly all sides. Prior to the epidemic, his nerves had become frazzled from obsessive, day-and-night study of his law books.

He had even put his own health at risk through personal neglect, leading to his emaciated appearance. One resident commented, "His best friends were afraid that he would craze himself—make himself derange[d]."[3]

And their fears *ultimately came true.* Lincoln failed to heed the call of Scripture to ...

> "Be alert and of sober mind
> so that you may pray."
> (1 Peter 4:7)

STRESS IS …

▶ **External pressure** causing physical, mental, or emotional strain

- "The stress from that heavy truck caused the old wooden bridge to collapse."

  "People cry out under a load of oppression; they plead for relief from the arm of the powerful" (Job 35:9).

▶ **Self-induced internal pressure** causing physical, mental, emotional, or spiritual strain

- "The stress of striving for perfectionism leaves me mentally and emotionally exhausted."

  "By one sacrifice he [God] has made perfect forever those who are being made holy" (Hebrews 10:14).

▶ **Internal resistance** responding to outside pressure

- "The stress in my lower back was caused by lifting heavy boxes."

  "My back is filled with searing pain; there is no health in my body" (Psalm 38:7).

▶ **Negative pressure** resulting in distress, danger, or destruction

- "The stress from many harsh winters destroyed the fruit trees in my back yard."

  "when calamity overtakes you like a storm, when disaster sweeps over you like a whirlwind, when distress and trouble overwhelm you" (Proverbs 1:27).

▶ **Positive pressure** producing motivation and movement

- "The stress of needing to support my family caused me to seek a better job."

    "The appetite of laborers works for them; their hunger drives them on" (Proverbs 16:26).

WHAT IS Unhealthy Stress?

Lincoln's life was battered and bruised by unhealthy stress, and the untimely death of Anna Mayes Rutledge dealt the final blow to his fragile and frail emotional and mental states.

It was cold and wet the day of Anna's funeral, and Lincoln was distressed about rain falling on her grave. Throughout Lincoln's life, cold, gloomy weather would be detrimental to his emotional health, often serving as the culminating factor to push him over the edge. He once wrote that bad weather had proved "to be very severe on defective nerves."[4]

Following Anna's death, Lincoln was seen wandering in nearby woods, gun in hand, admittedly contemplating suicide. Some friends literally locked him up inside their home to prevent him from killing himself.

It was around this time that yet another word was starting to be murmured about Lincoln: *crazy*.

And it was during this time that the Lord of peace described in 2 Thessalonians seemed to elude him:

> "Now may the Lord of peace himself give you peace at all times and in every way."
> (2 Thessalonians 3:16)

UNHEALTHY STRESS ...

▶ **Refers** more to the duration of stress over a considerable period of time

▶ **Includes** external or internal pressure that God does not intend for us to experience

▶ **Causes** detrimental effects to the body, as well as to the soul and spirit

▶ **Stretches** us beyond the threshold of our physical, mental, and emotional limits that God established within us to protect from overload

▶ **Plunges** us past a saturation point where nothing can be added without something else being eliminated

King Solomon, known for his wisdom, wrote ...

> "I saw the tears of the oppressed—
> and they have no comforter;
> power was on the side of their oppressors—
> and they have no comforter."
> (Ecclesiastes 4:1)

Post-Traumatic Stress Disorder

Post-traumatic stress disorder (PTSD) develops when someone fails to heal from a single traumatic event or a series of disturbing experiences. PTSD is generally revealed by characteristic symptoms following an extremely traumatic event (for example, childhood sexual or physical abuse, violent physical or sexual assault, war, terrorism, natural disaster, or car accident) that threatens loss of life or serious injury to a person or a loved one.[5]

▶ **Responding**. The response to the traumatic event involves intense fear, anxiety, helplessness, or horror, along with intrusive thoughts and persistent reoccurrence of the traumatic event through dreams or vivid memories.[6]

▶ **Avoiding**. Typically, a person will avoid anything associated with the trauma and will experience numbing of general responsiveness to life.[7]

Post-trauma sufferers haven't had the luxury of time to grieve losses or wrap their heads around what has happened to them because they are still "dodging bullets"—real or imaginary. Like soldiers fighting on a battlefield when their buddies fall at their sides, they can't stop, arrange proper burials, plan memorial services, and attend grief counseling. They are still fighting for their own lives.

The path out of PTSD involves intentionally stopping—mentally turning and emotionally heading back through the trauma—not to experience it again, but to process it and move on in a new direction.

For severe symptoms of PTSD, seek counseling. Process the flashbacks, dreams, nightmares, and other troubling experiences with a trained professional. If depression becomes severe or chronic, inform a medical doctor.

Those who face their pain and focus on their suffering through the healing process can say with the psalmist ...

"My comfort in my suffering is this:
Your promise preserves my life."
(Psalm 119:50)

WHAT DOES Scripture Say about Stress?

As a young boy, Abraham Lincoln was grounded in Scripture. His mother, Nancy, would set him on her lap and proceed to read from the family Bible.

The Ten Commandments were a focal passage, evidenced by Nancy's final words to her nine-year-old son: "Abe, I'm going to leave you now and I shall not return. I want you to be kind to your father and live as I have taught you. Love your heavenly Father and keep His commandments."[8]

Lincoln's mother died in her mid-thirties from an infectious disease known as "milk sick," stemming from a poisonous root eaten by cattle.

Lincoln's stepmother, Sarah Bush, built upon the young boy's spiritual foundation by faithfully taking him and his sister to Pigeon Creek Hard Shell Baptist Church every Sunday. Lincoln *heard* the Word of God, Lincoln *read* the Word of God, but there is no evidence until later in life that he turned to Scripture to find solace from his stress.

Lincoln's early experience is similar to that of King Asa of Judah:

"Though his disease was severe,
even in his illness he did not seek help from
the Lord, but only from the physicians."
(2 Chronicles 16:12)

▶ **Distress** "implies an external and usually temporary cause of great physical or mental strain and stress."[9]

"There will be trouble and distress for every human being who does evil ... " (Romans 2:9).

▶ **Distress** can be the result of severe, self-induced, internal stress.

"See, LORD, how distressed I am! I am in torment within, and in my heart I am disturbed, for I have been most rebellious" (Lamentations 1:20).

▶ **Distress** is a state of anguish, vexation, or affliction.

"While Paul was waiting for them in Athens, he was greatly distressed to see that the city was full of idols" (Acts 17:16).

▶ **Distress** is a word used over 100 times in the Bible (NIV) to describe negative stress.

- It most often pictures the negative result that pressure and pain can have on the heart.

  EXAMPLE: The apostle Paul wrote to those whom he deeply loved in the young Corinthian church—those who had severely rebelled against him, but had later sincerely repented.

  "For I wrote you out of great distress and anguish of heart and with many tears, not to grieve you but to let you know the depth of my love for you" (2 Corinthians 2:4).

▶ **Distress** is often a translation from the Hebrew word *tsarah*, which means "straits, distress."[10]

- The word means distress, anguish, or affliction in a spiritual or psychological sense.

  EXAMPLE: Due to the jealous rage of Joseph's 10 older brothers, his life was in severe jeopardy. And despite his distressful pleas, the brothers sold him as a slave and he was carted off to Egypt.

  Years later, the brothers found themselves in the depth of distress. Because of the severe famine in Israel, the brothers traveled to Egypt in an attempt to buy grain. But when they found themselves in a stressful predicament, they reflected on what they had done to Joseph many years before and wondered if their cruel treatment of Joseph was the cause of their distress.

  "We saw how distressed he [Joseph] was when he pleaded with us for his life, but we would not listen; that is why this distress has come on us."
  (Genesis 42:21)

CHARACTERISTICS

Abraham Lincoln's voracious study of his law books paid off with a prominent law practice and undergirded him for a lengthy political career.

For 30 years he literally dotted the political landscape: *elections, defeats, elections, defeats.* Lincoln's political career began in 1834 when he was elected to the Illinois State Legislature, and it had been a robust time to run for office. The state's economy was booming, its population had tripled in 10 years, and an $11 million internal improvements package had just passed to build roads, canals, and railroads.

An overall sense of optimism permeated throughout the state, but the economic boom eventually became a bust, and multiple stresses both personally and professionally led to Lincoln's second emotional collapse.

Scripture addresses the source of both good times and bad:

"Consider what God has done:
Who can straighten what he has made
crooked? When times are good, be happy;
but when times are bad, consider this:
God has made the one as well as the other."
(Ecclesiastes 7:13–14)

Abraham Lincoln referred to it as "that fatal first of Jany. 41."[11]

The date to which Lincoln referred is January 1, 1841, and even today a great deal of mystery surrounds precisely what event or events drove him to a breakdown. It's clear there were multiple stressors in his life both personally and professionally, but historians can only conjecture as to what indeed pushed him over the edge.

The once bustling Illinois economy had come to a disastrous standstill by the end of 1840. The internal improvements package to which Lincoln had so closely aligned himself was a failure, state debt exceeded $13.6 million, and bank-issued currency had lost all value. Lincoln's reputation was tanking along with the economy, and that was a bitter pill to swallow for a man who so highly valued character and a strong public presence.[12]

Like Lincoln, the apostle Paul faced multiple stressors. But, *unlike* young Lincoln, Paul entrusted himself to God and triumphed over stress.

> "We are hard pressed on every side,
> but not crushed;
> perplexed, but not in despair;
> persecuted, but not abandoned;
> struck down, but not destroyed."
> (2 Corinthians 4:8–9)

As we live day-in-day-out, we will all have varying amounts of stress. Contrary to what many think, a moderate amount of stress can be very helpful. For a student, the moderate stress of an exam typically provides the motivation to study.

Likewise, with no homework to turn in and no regular tests to take, many students would be unmotivated to study. If, however, there is too much stress, the possibility of burnout is ever present.

▶ **STAGE 1: No Light. Insufficient Stress.**

No motivation to move responsibly.

▶ **STAGE 2: Green Light. Positive Stress.**

Motivation to move responsibly.

▶ **STAGE 3: Yellow Light. Negative Stress.**

Motivational warning signs to slow down movement.

▶ **STAGE 4: Red Light. Burnout.**

Movement stops and repair is necessary.

"Those who disregard discipline despise themselves, but the one who heeds correction gains understanding."
(Proverbs 15:32)

"Lincoln," one observer noted, "went crazy as a loon."[13]

Razors had to be removed from his room, knives and other sharp objects had to be taken away from him. Lincoln was reeling, fears of a further tarnished reputation consumed him, but it was affairs of the heart—not affairs of the state—that sent his emotions into overdrive.

Lincoln was engaged to a young woman named Mary Todd, but his heart belonged to another, a graceful, curly-haired blonde named Matilda Edwards. Mary recognized Lincoln's affections for Matilda and eventually released him from the engagement, but not without exacting a significant amount of guilt upon the lovelorn Lincoln.

And many believe it was the breakup of Mary Todd that was the catalyst for "that fatal first of Jany. 41" for Lincoln's conscience was deeply stressed over the fact that his heart would wander while under a matrimonial agreement.

Lincoln could relate to the psalmist:

> "My guilt has overwhelmed me
> like a burden too heavy to bear."
> (Psalm 38:4)

▶ Stage 1: No Light

With insufficient stress to encourage an individual to act responsibly, you will find that the person ...

- Avoids responsibility
- Has poor relationships
- Is not productive
- Has no energy
- Experiences depression
- Has no purpose
- Lacks perspective on life
- Has a short temper

"Why, my soul, are you downcast? Why so disturbed within me? Put your hope in God, for I will yet praise him, my Savior and my God. My soul is downcast within me ... " (Psalm 42:5–6).

▶ Stage 2: Green Light

Positive stress pushes you to proper maintenance. When there is sufficient positive stress, you will find that a person ...

- Faces responsibility
- Is productive
- Is peaceful
- Is energetic
- Is enthusiastic
- Has responsible relationships
- Has fulfillment of purpose
- Has a positive perspective

"Now finish the work, so that your eager willingness to do it may be matched by your completion of it, according to your means" (2 Corinthians 8:11).

▶ STAGE 3: Yellow Light

That "check engine" light is sending the signal that something serious is occurring. The warning signs of stress are like the amber lights on a traffic signal—they caution you to be on the alert, to slow down, and to be prepared for upcoming change. The physical warning signs of stress can be ...

- Tension headaches, stomach aches
- Muscle aches, back aches
- Heavy sighing, rapid breathing
- High blood pressure
- Hyperalertness, anxiousness
- Restlessness, weight gain or loss
- Loss of sleep, excessive sleep
- Lack of concentration, constant worrying
- Indecisiveness, poor judgment
- Irritability, agitation

"Better a poor but wise youth than an old but foolish king who no longer knows how to heed a warning" (Ecclesiastes 4:13).

▶ STAGE 4: Red Light

Burnout is certainly not God's will for you. It may just be that you have not processed the stresses of life in a godly way. Instead of living at Stage 2, a person becomes ...

- Overwhelmed by responsibility
- Withdrawn from relationships
- Minimally productive
- Depressed (lack of enthusiasm), moody
- Purposeless, disinterested in sex
- Without perspective, but with erratic eating and sleeping patterns
- Easily fatigued, nervous

WHAT IS a Checklist for Burnout?

Lincoln was a man committed to honor and integrity, and his turbulent emotions concerning the breakup with Mary Todd can be traced in part to the gravity of a matrimonial contract in 19th century America. Legally binding, the rejected party even had the right to seek damages. Lincoln himself had successfully served as the attorney in a "breach of promise" suit.

Looking to the source, getting below the surface, the weightiness of a marriage pledge in the mid-1800s may also have contributed to "that fatal first of Jany. 41."

Following the breakup Lincoln continued on in a cathartic state of self-analysis, losing confidence in his ability to maintain resolve since he hadn't followed through and married Mary Todd.

Lincoln wrote to his longtime friend Joshua Speed: "I must regain my confidence in my own ability to keep my resolves when they are made. In that ability you know, I once prided myself as the only, or at least the chief, gem of my character; that gem I lost—how, and when, you too well know. I have not yet regained it; and until I do, I cannot trust myself in any matter of much importance."[14]

On November 4, 1842, Abraham Lincoln did end up marrying Mary Todd, and one observer noted he "looked and acted as if he was going to the Slaughter."[15]

Character came at a high cost to Lincoln, similar to a sacrificial call of Scripture:

"Whoever wants to be my disciple must deny themselves and take up their cross daily and follow me."
(Luke 9:23)

Checklist for Burnout

Emotional Symptoms

☐ I am plagued with guilt over not being as responsible or committed as I should be.

☐ I feel apathetic and anxious.

☐ I feel depressed.

☐ I feel I don't do things as well as I could and should.

☐ I have a great deal of self-doubt.

☐ I have a sense of helplessness.

☐ I have a sense of hopelessness.

☐ I have decreased self-esteem.

☐ I have difficulty concentrating.

☐ I have feelings of confusion.

☐ I have feelings of disenchantment.

☐ I have feelings of disorientation.

☐ I have feelings of disillusionment or failure.

☐ I have increased irritability.

☐ I have less time and energy for relationships.

☐ I have uncharacteristic anger, cynicism, and negativism.

Physical Symptoms

☐ I am susceptible to almost every cold and virus.

☐ I eat and snack excessively.

☐ I feel tired and lifeless most of the time.

☐ I generally feel nervous and unsettled.

☐ I grind my teeth at night.

- ☐ I have a rapid pulse.
- ☐ I have allergies or asthma.
- ☐ I have difficulty relaxing.
- ☐ I have frequent, severe headaches.
- ☐ I have high blood pressure.
- ☐ I have indigestion often.
- ☐ I have lost or gained a lot of weight.
- ☐ I have lower back pain.
- ☐ I have shortness of breath.
- ☐ I have tightness in my neck and shoulders.
- ☐ I have trouble sleeping at night.
- ☐ I often have cold hands and sweating palms.
- ☐ I often have diarrhea or constipation.

Spiritual Symptoms

- ☐ I am apathetic toward Scripture.
- ☐ I am feeling more and more desperate to improve my situation.
- ☐ I am losing confidence in God to help me.
- ☐ I fail to recognize my own limits much of the time.
- ☐ I feel I am in a spiritual vacuum.
- ☐ I feel I am on my own.
- ☐ I feel I have lost perspective on life.
- ☐ I feel God has given up on me.
- ☐ I feel like giving up on myself.
- ☐ I rarely pray or have quiet time anymore.

No one will likely experience all these symptoms, but if you checked four or more, you may need to evaluate how you are responding to the pressures in your life. You may also need to check with a health-care professional.

Are you releasing your heavy load to the Lord and allowing His peace to permeate your heart?

The Bible says ...

"A heart at peace gives life to the body ..."
(Proverbs 14:30)

CAUSES

While there is widespread speculation that Abraham Lincoln's initial breakup with Mary Todd prompted the "fatal first," there was no shortage of other stressful events in Lincoln's life that could have contributed to his emotional breakdown.

January 1, 1841, was the date that Joshua Speed ended his business ties in Springfield, Illinois, and Lincoln faced the prospect that his loyal, longtime companion might move away. And there could have been someone else precious to Lincoln accompanying Speed. On the final evening of the leap year of 1840, there was a tradition for men to propose marriage.

It appears that Matilda Edwards captured the heart of another besides Lincoln—Joshua Speed. Did Lincoln learn of a proposal that fateful "fatal first"[6] In the midst of so much stress, there was One to whom Lincoln later turned, but not in January 1841.

"When hard pressed, I cried to the LORD;
he brought me into a spacious place."
(Psalm 118:5)

The seven classic causes of stress worked in conjunction to bring emotional upheaval to Lincoln's life.

January 1, 1841, posed yet another looming deadline for Lincoln. It was the final date for the state of Illinois to pay back $175,000 in debt interest. The legislature had met in special session and determined that if the state couldn't pay, it would enter into receivership. The "fatal first" for Lincoln may have been tied to financial fears.

The debt crisis had already weakened him politically; would it now render him powerless? Like Job, whose reputation plummeted following attacks by Satan, Lincoln no doubt longed for the days when his name was revered and respected.

"When I went to the gate of the city
and took my seat in the public square,
the young men saw me and stepped aside
and the old men rose to their feet;
the chief men refrained from speaking
and covered their mouths with their hands."
(Job 29:7–9)

CONFLICT[17]

▶ **Reasons you can experience conflict:**

- Opposing values of family and friends
- Unresolved anger in relationships

- Unrealistic expectations of another person
- Lack of open communication in relationships

Paul was met with extreme opposition from others.

"Are they servants of Christ? (I am out of my mind to talk like this.) I am more. I have worked much harder, been in prison more frequently, been flogged more severely, and been exposed to death again and again. Five times I received from the Jews the forty lashes minus one" (2 Corinthians 11:23–24).

CRISIS

▶ **Reasons you can experience crisis:**

- Death of a friend or family member
- Separation or divorce
- Severe illness or sudden handicap
- Unexpected trauma of any kind

Paul was shipwrecked and often in extreme danger.

"Three times I was beaten with rods, once I was pelted with stones, three times I was shipwrecked, I spent a night and a day in the open sea, I have been constantly on the move. I have been in danger from rivers, in danger from bandits, in danger from my fellow Jews, in danger from Gentiles; in danger in the city, in danger in the country, in danger at sea; and in danger from false believers" (2 Corinthians 11:25–26).

CHANGE

▶ **Reasons you can go through change:**

- Change in environment or employment
- Change in financial or marital status
- Change in cultural or spiritual values
- Change in sleeping and health habits

Paul was constantly on the move, often going without sleep.

"I have been constantly on the move. ... I have labored and toiled and have often gone without sleep; I have known hunger and thirst and have often gone without food; I have been cold and naked" (2 Corinthians 11:26–27).

CONDEMNATION

▶ **Reasons you can experience condemnation:**

- Rejection by significant others
- Lack of support from coworkers
- Betrayal of a friend
- False accusations by family members

Paul was rejected and betrayed by the Gentiles and by his own people.

"I have been in danger from rivers, in danger from bandits, in danger from my fellow Jews, in danger from Gentiles; in danger in the city, in danger in the country, in danger at sea; and in danger from false believers" (2 Corinthians 11:26).

CONCERNS

▶ **Reasons you can carry concern:**

- Unsaved or rebellious loved ones
- Unpredictable or uncertain future
- Recent or frequent fear of failures
- Perfectionism or excessive attention to details

Paul carried the daily pressure of concern for the churches.

"Besides everything else, I face daily the pressure of my concern for all the churches" (2 Corinthians 11:28).

COMPETITION

▶ **Reasons you can experience competition:**

- Self-acceptance based on superior performance
- Comparisons between family, friends, or coworkers
- Envy or jealousy among neighbors or business associates
- Significance or security based on outperforming others

Paul chose to boast only in his weaknesses.

"If I must boast, I will boast of the things that show my weakness" (2 Corinthians 11:30).

Conscience

▶ **Reasons you can challenge conscience:**

- Self, others, or things seem more important than God.
- Self-effort is perceived as the best way of meeting needs.
- Personal needs eclipse the needs of others.
- Acknowledgement of sin is considered an admission of weakness.

Paul was secure in his integrity before the Lord.

"The God and Father of the Lord Jesus, who is to be praised forever, knows that I am not lying" (2 Corinthians 11:31).

WHAT PRESSURES Increase Stress?

Uncertain circumstances increased stress in Lincoln's life, but there was that one constant that could be counted on to drag him down to the emotional dregs, that one season of the year that continually blew a chill across the tormented man's soul. Winter, 1840–1841, had been *unusually* bitterly cold.

A friend of Lincoln's said it was colder in Illinois than anyone could remember, and a newcomer to the state made the following observation: "I am sure I have seen colder weather in Connecticut. But I have never seen a place where cold is to be dreaded so much."[18]

Lincoln was accustomed to that "dread," and it powerfully impacted his emotions each and every year. Oh that the troubled man would have warmed his spirit and soul with this glorious assurance:

> "The LORD is God, and he has
> made his light shine on us."
> (Psalm 118:27)

YOUR MENTAL RESPONSE

▶ **Mental stress** is caused by the way you think about or interpret events.[19]

- If you dwell on losing your job, you will feel stress.
- If you dwell on God's faithfulness to provide, He will replace your stress with His peace.

Do you have a positive or a negative outlook? If you dwell on negative thoughts, you can turn almost anything, even good circumstances, into stress. This is why God wants you to meditate on what is pure and good.

The Bible says about the Lord: *"You will keep in perfect peace those whose minds are steadfast, because they trust in you"* (Isaiah 26:3).

YOUR EMOTIONAL RESPONSE

▶ **Emotional stress** is caused by the way you process your thoughts.[20]

- If you think bitter thoughts, you will feel bitter emotions.

- If you think forgiving thoughts, you will feel forgiveness in your heart.

Although feelings need to be recognized and acknowledged, they are basically a product of your thinking, and they can be controlled. Emotional immaturity makes you a prisoner to your feelings and keeps you chained to undue stress.

Jesus said, *"Peace I leave with you; my peace I give you. I do not give to you as the world gives. Do not let not your hearts be troubled and do not be afraid"* (John 14:27).

Your Physical Response

▶ **Physical stress** is caused by the way your body automatically responds to external pressure.[21]

- If you mentally dwell on your difficulties, you can develop physical fatigue.
- If you trust God for His timing, He provides you peace—mental, emotional, and physical peace.

If pressure is not dealt with in a healthy way, you become susceptible to a variety of physical problems. Prolonged stress can result in harmful physical reactions, such as elevated blood pressure and increased cholesterol levels. The Bible reveals that many of the consequences of stress can be avoided if you keep His Word in your heart.

"Do not let them [God's words of wisdom] *out of your sight, keep them within your heart; for they are life to those who find them and health to one's whole body"* (Proverbs 4:21–22).

Your Spiritual Response

▶ **Spiritual stress** is caused by the way you view God, His involvement in your life, and His sovereignty over your life.

- If you believe God is indifferent to you and powerless to work in your life and circumstances, you will have a crisis of faith.

- If you believe Him to be a loving Father, Helper, Friend, and Healer with infinite power to work on your behalf, you will enter into His rest and receive His peace.

The Lord states His perfect plan through the prophet Isaiah: *"My people will live in peaceful dwelling places, in secure homes, in undisturbed places of rest"* (Isaiah 32:18).

WHAT STRESSORS Can Cause Stress and Distress?

Stress is an individualistic, subjective experience because what one person finds stressful another person may find invigorating. Situations and pressures that cause stress are often referred to as stressors, and while life-changing events cause major stress, it is the hassles that occur on a daily basis that impact people the most.

Although David did not experience all of the stressors we have today, he certainly had his share of troubles that would create intense if not almost unbearable distress for anyone, anytime, and anywhere.

> "Be merciful to me, my God,
> for my enemies are in hot pursuit;
> all day long they press their attack.
> My adversaries pursue me all day long;
> in their pride many are attacking me. ...
> All day long they twist my words;
> all their schemes are for my ruin.
> They conspire, they lurk, they watch
> my steps, hoping to take my life."
> (Psalm 56:1–2, 5–6)

Some examples of typical stressors include:

▶ **Life transitions**

- Learning to crawl, walk, talk
- Being potty trained, making friends, sharing with others
- Having unmet needs, wants, desires
- Dealing with siblings, attending school, dating
- Going to college, getting a job, getting married
- Moving, buying a house, having children
- Receiving a promotion, changing jobs, losing a job
- Experiencing an empty nest, infidelity, divorce, widowhood
- Taking care of elderly parents, illness, disability
- Retiring, poor health, grieving the death of significant others

▶ **Daily hassles**

- Dealing with deadlines, demands, difficult people

- Encountering traffic, road rage, office politics
- Exhausting work, social schedule, church commitments
- Meeting needs of family, friends, employers
- Making phone calls, writing e-mails
- Planning schedules, preparing meals, staying in shape
- Running errands, paying bills, resolving family problems
- Taking care of cars, doing house repairs, maintaining a yard
- Buying clothes, stocking up on supplies, helping children with homework
- Misplacing keys, losing wallet, losing sleep

▶ **Internal factors**

- Fearing the uncertainties of life
- Engaging in negative self-talk
- Nurturing a pessimistic outlook
- Exhibiting a critical spirit
- Lacking faith in a loving, all-powerful God
- Entertaining unrealistic expectations
- Maintaining unforgiveness
- Resenting responsibilities
- Possessing phobias or addictions
- Harboring anger

▶ **Individual differences**

- Avoiding crowds vs. enjoying crowds
- Fearing the spotlight vs. craving the spotlight

- Collapsing under pressure vs. thriving under pressure
- Eluding confrontation vs. embracing confrontation
- Disliking caretaking vs. liking caretaking
- Monopolizing conversations vs. minimizing conversations
- Dodging physical activity vs. pursuing physical activity
- Evading problems vs. creating problems
- Pleasing others vs. pleasing self
- Preferring to follow vs. preferring to lead

In reality, there are innumerable possible stressors in life because any event that is considered threatening, difficult to manage, or producing excessive pressure can result in stress. Individual beliefs, attitudes, interpretations, perceptions, and experiences influence what becomes stressful to a particular individual.

Therefore, it is critical that the first signs of stress or distress be met with a reality check. Identifying the truth behind our reactions to events in life is the starting place for turning destructive distress into constructive action. The psalmist clearly shows how important truth is to God:

> "Behold, You desire truth in the inward
> parts, and in the hidden part
> You will make me to know wisdom."
> (Psalm 51:6 NKJV)

You must rally or die.

Joshua Speed, the ever-concerned friend, had witnessed Lincoln respond negatively to severe stress in his life time and time again, so he challenged him following his second breakdown to respond differently rather than desperately. It became a pivotal chapter in Lincoln's life, an awakening that stirred Lincoln to aspire to greatness.

Lincoln told Speed that he was not afraid to die, but he had an "irrepressible desire" to make a great contribution to the people of his generation, to "so impress himself upon them as to link his name with something that would redound to the interest of his fellow man."[22]

Lincoln was beginning to move from a wrong belief about stress to a right belief about stress, and one day he would turn to God to help him carry the crushing burden of an entire nation. His desire to serve others is a consistent call of Scripture.

> " ... serve one another humbly in love.
> For the entire law is fulfilled
> in keeping this one command:
> 'Love your neighbor as yourself.'"
> (Galatians 5:13–14)

▶ Wrong Belief:

"My life is out of control. I feel helpless to cope with all this stress in my life."

Right Belief:

"God has allowed this stress in my life to bless me and to reveal my weaknesses. I am grateful for the pressures that have pressed me closer to Him and caused me to allow Christ to be my strength."

"'My [Jesus'] grace is sufficient for you,
for my power is made perfect in weakness.'
Therefore I [Paul] will boast all the more
gladly about my weaknesses,
so that Christ's power may rest on me.
That is why, for Christ's sake, I delight in
weaknesses, in insults, in hardships,
in persecutions, in difficulties.
For when I am weak, then I am strong."
(2 Corinthians 12:9–10)

FOUR POINTS OF GOD'S PLAN

#1 God's Purpose for You is *Salvation*.

What was God's motivation in sending Jesus Christ to earth?

To express His love for you by saving you!

The Bible says ...

"God so loved the world that he gave his one and only Son, that whoever believes in him shall not perish but have eternal life. For God did not send his Son into the world to condemn the world, but to save the world through him" (John 3:16–17).

What was Jesus' purpose in coming to earth?

To forgive your sins, to empower you to have victory over sin, and to enable you to live a fulfilled life! Jesus said ...

"I have come that they may have life, and that they may have it more abundantly" (John 10:10 NKJV).

#2 Your Problem is *Sin*.

What exactly is sin?

Sin is living independently of God's standard— knowing what is right, but choosing what is wrong. The Bible says ...

"If anyone, then, knows the good they ought to do and doesn't do it, it is sin for them" (James 4:17).

What is the major consequence of sin?

Spiritual death, eternal separation from God. Scripture states ...

"Your iniquities [sins] *have separated you from your God"* (Isaiah 59:2).

"The wages of sin is death, but the gift of God is eternal life in Christ Jesus our Lord" (Romans 6:23).

#3 God's Provision for You is the *Savior.*

Can anything remove the penalty for sin?

Yes! Jesus died on the cross to personally pay the penalty for your sins. The Bible says ...

"God demonstrates his own love for us in this: While we were still sinners, Christ died for us" (Romans 5:8).

What is the solution to being separated from God?

Belief in (entrusting your life to) Jesus Christ as the only way to God the Father. Jesus says ...

"I am the way and the truth and the life. No one comes to the Father except through me" (John 14:6).

"Believe in the Lord Jesus, and you will be saved" (Acts 16:31).

#4 Your Part is *Surrender.*

Give Christ control of your life, entrusting yourself to Him.

"Jesus said to his disciples, 'Whoever wants to be my disciple must deny themselves and take up their

cross [die to your own self-rule] *and follow me. For whoever wants to save their life will lose it, but whoever loses their life for me will find it. What good will it be for someone to gain the whole world, yet forfeit their soul?"* (Matthew 16:24–26).

Place your faith in (rely on) Jesus Christ as your personal Lord and Savior and reject your "good works" as a means of earning God's approval.

"It is by grace you have been saved, through faith—and this is not from yourselves, it is the gift of God—not by works, so that no one can boast."
(Ephesians 2:8–9)

The moment you choose to receive Jesus as your Lord and Savior—entrusting your life to Him—He comes to live inside you. Then He gives you His power to live the fulfilled life God has planned for you.

If you want to be fully forgiven by God and become the person God created you to be, you can tell Him in a simple, heartfelt prayer like this:

PRAYER OF SALVATION

"God, I want a real relationship with You.
I admit that many times
I've chosen to go my own way
instead of Your way.
Please forgive me for my sins.
Jesus, thank You for dying on the cross
to pay the penalty for my sins.
Come into my life to be my Lord
and my Savior.
Change me from the inside out
and make me the person
You created me to be.
In Your holy name I pray. Amen."

WHAT CAN YOU NOW EXPECT?

If you sincerely prayed this prayer, look at what God says!

Accepting Jesus as your Lord and Savior does not make you immune to the stresses of life. But with Jesus living inside of you, His strength helps you because *"He gives strength to the weary and increases the power of the weak"* (Isaiah 40:29).

STEPS TO SOLUTION

Although Abraham Lincoln would struggle with stress and dark, desperate emotions his entire life, the sense of "greater purpose" set him on a course that would not only protect him from having another breakdown, but put him in the national spotlight.

As the 1860 presidential race geared up, one topic dominated the political conversation: *slavery.* That line in the sand clearly divided the north from the south. Lincoln was becoming increasingly recognized for his political skill and savvy, and his name recognition began to extend beyond the Illinois borders. There were three criteria the Republican candidate had to meet: He had to be a "man of the people," a solid advocate of antislavery, and a politician without even a hint of radicalism.[23]

To an increasing number in the Republican Party, Abraham Lincoln was that man, and it truly began to appear that the favor of God was resting upon the congressman from Illinois.

"No one from the east or the west or from
the desert can exalt themselves.
It is God who judges:
He brings one down, he exalts another."
(Psalm 75:6–7)

Key Verses to Memorize

In 1860, Abraham Lincoln was elected president of the *United* States of America, but *division* was already in the air. Southerners considered the election of a stalwart antislavery candidate a signal—it's time to secede—and not a moment's time was wasted. About 10,000 volunteer soldiers were recruited and equipped in South Carolina; the state of Georgia put $1 million on the table to fund a war; and Louisiana approved $500,000 for guns and confederate fighters.[24]

The newly-elected President Abraham Lincoln would not only be stressed, but *"weary and burdened"* as Scripture describes, from day one. But now he had a Burden-Bearer to lighten his heavy load and give rest to his troubled soul.

> *"Come to me, all you who are weary*
> *and burdened, and I will give you rest.*
> *Take my yoke upon you*
> *and learn from me,*
> *for I am gentle and humble in heart,*
> *and you will find rest for your souls.*
> *For my yoke is easy*
> *and my burden is light."*
> (Matthew 11:28–30)

Before long, eight more states joined the initial trio that seceded and a full-scale civil war now painfully preoccupied the incoming president.

Like Elijah, Abraham Lincoln now found himself at his most desperate and distraught time seeking rest, guidance, and empowerment from God. Following a devastating Union army defeat at Fredericksburg, Virginia, Lincoln stressfully paced the floor of his office and moaned repeatedly in grief and anguish, "What has God put me in this place for?"[25]

The dressmaker of Lincoln's wife recounted an insightful turn of events concerning the dejected president's source of strength and solace. Lincoln, appearing even more stressed and burdened than usual, collapsed on a sofa and reached for a Bible. Within 15 minutes the dressmaker witnessed an incredible change in his countenance; hope and new resolve were written all over his face.

Curious as to what precisely Lincoln was reading, she subtly peered over his shoulder and quickly discovered—the book of Job.[26] Lincoln seemingly had found a kindred spirit with Job, a man like Elijah who too was well-acquainted with stress and suffering.

Even Elijah's name (meaning "Jehovah is God") announces that he is a messenger approved and sent by God. Elijah had significant spiritual strength, yet he ended up with an empty tank under a broom tree, begging God to deliver him from his great distress.

Elijah on Empty

1 Kings 19

▶ **Scripture Reveals the Cause of Elijah's Burnout.**

- **Elijah lost confidence in the sovereign power of God.**

"Elijah was afraid and ran for his life. When he came to Beersheba in Judah, he left his servant there" (v. 3).

- **Elijah had reached the end of his own resources.**

"... while he himself went a day's journey into the wilderness. He came to a broom bush, sat down under it and prayed that he might die. 'I have had enough, Lord,' he said. 'Take my life; I am no better than my ancestors'" (v. 4).

- **Elijah was tired and exhausted.**

"Then he lay down under the bush and fell asleep. All at once an angel touched him and said, 'Get up and eat'" (v. 5).

▶ **Scripture Tells Us the Steps God Used to Restore Elijah**

- **Elijah left his servant to be alone with God.**

"Elijah was afraid and ran for his life. When he came to Beersheba in Judah, he left his servant there, while he himself went a day's journey into the wilderness. He came to a broom bush, sat down under it and prayed that he might die. 'I have had enough, Lord,' he said. 'Take my life; I am no better than my ancestors'" (vv. 3–4).

- **Elijah received the rest and food provided by God.**

"Then he lay down under the bush and fell asleep. All at once an angel touched him and said, 'Get up and eat.' He looked around, and there by his head was some bread baked over hot coals, and a jar of water. He ate and drank and then lay down again. The angel of the LORD came back a second time and touched him and said, 'Get up and eat, for the journey is too much for you.' So he got up and ate and drank" (vv. 5–8).

- **Elijah moved forward with God's provision.**

"So he got up and ate and drank. Strengthened by that food, he traveled forty days and forty nights until he reached Horeb, the mountain of God" (v. 8).

- **God was not silent but asked Elijah to explain his need.**

"There he went into a cave and spent the night. And the word of the LORD came to him: 'What are you doing here, Elijah?'" (v. 9).

- **Elijah was honest with God about his feelings.**

"He replied, 'I have been very zealous for the LORD God Almighty. The Israelites have rejected your covenant, torn down your altars, and put your prophets to death with the sword. I am the only one left, and now they are trying to kill me too'" (v. 10).

- **God showed Elijah that He was still in control.**

"The LORD said, 'Go out and stand on the mountain in the presence of the LORD, for the LORD is about

to pass by.' Then a great and powerful wind tore the mountains apart and shattered the rocks before the LORD, but the LORD was not in the wind. After the wind there was an earthquake, but the LORD was not in the earthquake. After the earthquake came a fire, but the LORD was not in the fire" (vv. 11–12).*

- **God spoke to Elijah in a gentle whisper.**

"And after the fire came a gentle whisper. When Elijah heard it, he pulled his cloak over his face and went out and stood at the mouth of the cave. Then a voice said to him, 'What are you doing here, Elijah?'" (vv. 12–13).

- **Elijah's response revealed that he did not understand how God was working.**

"He replied, 'I have been very zealous for the LORD God Almighty. The Israelites have rejected your covenant, torn down your altars, and put your prophets to death with the sword. I am the only one left, and now they are trying to kill me too'" (v. 14).

- **God revealed the next steps for Elijah to take.**

"The LORD said to him, 'Go back the way you came, and go to the Desert of Damascus. When you get there, anoint Hazael king over Aram. Also anoint Jehu son of Nimshi king over Israel, and anoint Elisha son of Shaphat from Abel Meholah to succeed you as prophet'" (vv. 15–16).

- **God revealed part of His future plans to Elijah.**

"Jehu will put to death any who escape the sword of Hazael, and Elisha will put to death any who escape the sword of Jehu. Yet I reserve seven thousand in

Israel—all whose knees have not bowed to Baal and whose mouths have not kissed him" (vv. 17–18).

- **Elijah obeyed God and went back to the job God had given him.**

"So Elijah went from there and found Elisha son of Shaphat. He was plowing with twelve yoke of oxen, and he himself was driving the twelfth pair. Elijah went up to him and threw his cloak around him" (v. 19).

- **God gave Elijah the gift of a genuine friend and companion.**

"Elisha then left his oxen and ran after Elijah. 'Let me kiss my father and mother goodbye,' he said, 'and then I will come with you.' 'Go back,' Elijah replied. 'What have I done to you?' So Elisha left him and went back. He took his yoke of oxen and slaughtered them. He burned the plowing equipment to cook the meat and gave it to the people, and they ate. Then he set out to follow Elijah and became his servant" (vv. 20–21).

God sometimes allows difficult situations in your life to increase your reliance on Him and to form a stronger relationship with Him. The events in which Elijah found himself were beyond his control and demanded a complete dependence on God. If your prayer life is to penetrate to the deeper layers of your faith, you may find yourself under the broom tree of a broken spirit. *"In my distress I called to the Lord; I cried to my God for help. From his temple he heard my voice; my cry came before him, into his ears."* (Psalm 18:6)

REACHING THE TARGET: TRANSFORMATION!

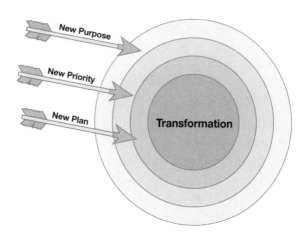

THE FREEDOM FORMULA

	A New Purpose
+	A New Priority
+	A New Plan
	A Transformed Life

▶ **Target #1—A New Purpose**: God's purpose for me is to be conformed to the character of Christ.

"Those God foreknew he also predestined to be conformed to the image of his Son" (Romans 8:29).

- "I'll do whatever it takes to be conformed to the character of Christ."

▶ **Target #2—A New Priority**: God's priority for me is to change my thinking.

"Do not conform to the pattern of this world, but be transformed by the renewing of your mind" (Romans 12:2).

- "I'll do whatever it takes to line up my thinking with God's thinking.

▶ **Target #3—A New Plan**: God's plan for me is to rely on Christ's strength, not my strength, to be all He created me to be.

"I can do all things through him who strengthens me" (Philippians 4:13 ESV).

- "I'll do whatever it takes to fulfill His plan in His strength."

My Personalized Plan

▶ **Receive** God's rest and physical nourishment.

- I will get at least eight hours of refreshing sleep each night.
- I will make an effort to start eating healthy meals and snacks.

"He makes me lie down in green pastures, he leads me beside quiet waters, he refreshes my soul" (Psalm 23:2–3).

▶ **Move** forward with God's provision.

- I will increase my dependence on God for my daily needs.
- I will pray for all the poor and hungry around the world.

"I know what it is to be in need, and I know what it

is to have plenty. I have learned the secret of being content in any and every situation, whether well fed or hungry, whether living in plenty or in want" (Philippians 4:12).

▶ **Wait** on God's response.

- I will not get ahead of God with hasty decisions, but I will strive to walk with Him.
- I will pray for the Holy Spirit's discernment.

"Wait for the LORD; be strong and take heart and wait for the LORD" (Psalm 27:14).

▶ **Communicate** honestly with God.

- I will truthfully tell God what I need.
- I will faithfully thank Him for all He has done.

"Do not be anxious about anything, but in every situation, by prayer and petition, with thanksgiving, present your requests to God" (Philippians 4:6).

▶ **Place** your trust in God, giving Him control.

- I will surrender my will to God's will.
- I will trust God with every detail of my life.

"But those who hope in the LORD will renew their strength. They will soar on wings like eagles; they will run and not grow weary, they will walk and not be faint" (Isaiah 40:31).

▶ **Listen** for the gentle whisper of God.

- I will "be still" and allow God to speak to my heart.
- I will consciously slow down my hectic pace.

"Be still before the LORD and wait patiently for him" (Psalm 37:7).

▶ **Be patient** when you don't understand God's plan.

- I will trust God with every detail of my life.
- I will acknowledge that my Creator knows all my days.

"Be joyful in hope, patient in affliction, faithful in prayer" (Romans 12:12).

▶ **Rely** on instructions from God.

- I will read my Bible and allow God to teach me His ways.
- I will remember that God has my best interest at heart.

"I will instruct you and teach you in the way you should go; I will counsel you with my loving eye on you" (Psalm 32:8).

▶ **Obey** God despite your past difficulty.

- I will rest in God's forgiveness.
- I will begin again with God's help.

"Seek the LORD while he may be found; call on him while he is near. Let the wicked forsake their ways and the unrighteous their thoughts. Let them turn to the LORD, and he will have mercy on them, and to our God, for he will freely pardon" (Isaiah 55:6–7).

▶ **Be ready** for God's blessing.

- I will pray with expectation.
- I will cling to the promises of Scripture.

"Call to me and I will answer you and tell you great and unsearchable things you do not know" (Jeremiah 33:3).

Seasons of stress can become opportunities for evaluating our lives and values. Carefully considering how God is working and determining a wisest course of action can transform stress into a hidden blessing from God.

> "Give careful thought to the paths for your feet and be steadfast in all your ways."
> (Proverbs 4:26)

HOW TO Conquer Classic Causes of Stress

After you experience excessive wear and tear, and you know what conditions contribute to your stress, what action can you take? How can you conquer the classic causes of stress? If the pressure in your life is being used to press you closer to the Lord, then you can cease striving in an uphill battle.

> "This is a trustworthy saying
> that deserves full acceptance.
> That is why we labor and strive, because
> we have put our hope in the living God,
> who is the Savior of all people,
> and especially of those who believe."
> (1 Timothy 4:9–10)

CONFLICT

▶ **How you can conquer conflict:**

- Accept one another's differences and focus on common goals.
- Resolve past anger and let go of present grudges.
- Avoid unrealistic expectations of others.
- Speak openly and honestly in relationships.

Paul encouraged the church at Rome: *"May the God who gives endurance and encouragement give you the same attitude of mind toward each other that Christ Jesus had, so that with one mind and one voice you may glorify the God and Father of our Lord Jesus Christ. Accept one another, then, just as Christ accepted you, in order to bring praise to God"* (Romans 15:5–7).

CRISIS

▶ **How you can conquer crisis:**

- Accept God's sovereign rule over life and death.
- Trust God's leadership in all relationship difficulties.
- Depend on God's sufficiency in physical trials.
- Rely on God's comfort and peace when blindsided by trauma.

King David acknowledged the sovereignty of God in his own life: *"... all the days ordained for me were written in your book before one of them came to be"* (Psalm 139:16).

CHANGE

▶**How you can conquer change:**

- View change as natural, constant, and ordained by God.
- Accept unwelcome changes as occasions to deepen trust in God.
- Welcome change as an opportunity to learn and grow.
- Consider physical changes as challenges to conquer and develop Christlike character.

Daniel praised God as a change agent: *"Praise be to the name of God for ever and ever; wisdom and power are his. He changes times and seasons; he deposes kings and raises up others. He gives wisdom to the wise and knowledge to the discerning"* (Daniel 2:20–21).

CONDEMNATION

▶**How you can conquer condemnation:**

- Expect to be rejected just as Jesus was rejected.
- Cultivate a spirit of cooperation and teamwork.
- Maintain faithfulness in the face of unfaithfulness.
- Extend forgiveness and speak the truth.

Paul encouraged the early Christian church to walk in forgiveness: *"Bear with each other and forgive one another if any of you has a grievance against someone. Forgive as the Lord forgave you"* (Colossians 3:13).

CONCERNS

▶ **How you can conquer concerns:**

- Entrust loved ones to the Lord's care and protection.
- Trust God with tomorrow and enjoy life today.
- Learn from failures—they can be more valuable than successes.
- Put away perfectionism—focus on improvement while aiming for excellence.

Jesus addressed the concerns of life: *"So do not worry, saying, 'What shall we eat?' or 'What shall we drink?' or 'What shall we wear?' ... But seek first his kingdom and his righteousness, and all these things will be given to you as well. Therefore do not worry about tomorrow, for tomorrow will worry about itself"* (Matthew 6:31, 33–34).

COMPETITION

▶ **How you can conquer competition:**

- Base your personal acceptance on being accepted by Christ.
- Consider individual weaknesses as God's opportunities.
- Relinquish your desire for control to God's sovereignty.
- Derive joy from the success of others and the glorification of God.

Paul experienced competition from others who preached the Gospel: "... *some preach Christ out of envy and rivalry, but others out of goodwill.* ... *But what does it matter? The important thing is that in every way, whether from false motives or true, Christ is preached. And because of this I rejoice. Yes, and I will continue to rejoice*" (Philippians 1:15, 18).

CONSCIENCE

▶ **How you can conquer conscience:**

- Give God first place in every activity.
- Turn to God as the resource for meeting every need.
- Respond to the needs of others.
- Confess sinful thoughts and acts to God and change sinful ways.

Paul addressed the need of having and maintaining a clear conscience: "*I strive always to keep my conscience clear before God and man*" (Acts 24:16).

President Abraham Lincoln was a pursuer of truth, and he rejected the $4 billion[27] slave industry as a legitimate institution no matter how much stress his stance would produce. He made his first attack against slavery on the floor of the Illinois legislature almost 25 years before becoming president, and his famous Gettysburg Address three years into his presidency reinforced his unwavering commitment to perceive and treat people as God perceives and treats people—*as equals.*

Consider Lincoln's words when the Gettysburg battlefield was being dedicated as a national cemetery: "Fourscore and seven years ago our fathers brought forth on this continent a new nation conceived in liberty and dedicated to the proposition that all men are created equal. ... we here highly resolve that these dead shall not have died in vain—that this nation under God shall have a new birth of freedom—and that government of the people, by the people, for the people shall not perish from the earth."[28]

The apostle Paul described the equality and unity that all people have in Christ:

"So in Christ Jesus you are all children of God through faith, for all of you who were baptized into Christ have clothed yourselves with Christ. There is neither Jew nor Gentile, neither slave nor free, nor is there male and female, for you are all one in Christ Jesus."
(Galatians 3:26–28)

▶ **LIE #1: "The more I do for God, the more He will love me."**

TRUTH: God already loves you completely. Nothing you can do will increase His love for you.

"Are you so foolish? After beginning by means of the Spirit, are you now trying to finish by means of the flesh?" (Galatians 3:3).

▶ **LIE #2: "I will lose God's love if I fail."**

TRUTH: God's love is always with you regardless of what you do.

"For I am convinced that neither death nor life, neither angels nor demons, neither the present nor the future, nor any powers, neither height nor depth, nor anything else in all creation, will be able to separate us from the love of God that is in Christ Jesus our Lord" (Romans 8:38–39).

▶ **LIE #3: "When I'm not pleasing God, I feel His condemnation."**

TRUTH: God's heart for you is not condemnation. He desires freedom for you and condemns only the sin that has you in bondage.

"There is now no condemnation for those who are in Christ Jesus, because through Christ Jesus the law of the Spirit who gives life has set you free from the law of sin and death" (Romans 8:1–2).

▶ **LIE #4: "I'm afraid that if I fail, God will punish me."**

TRUTH: God does not punish us. He disciplines us for our good that we may share in His holiness.

"They disciplined us for a little while as they thought best; but God disciplines us for our good, in order that we may share his holiness" (Hebrews 12:10).

▶ **LIE #5: "Because God is always available when anyone needs Him, I should be too."**

TRUTH: Jesus was not always available. He consistently left the crowds and His disciples to be alone and pray.

"After leaving them, he went up on a mountainside to pray" (Mark 6:46).

▶ **LIE #6: "To burn out for a cause is admirable."**

TRUTH: God never applauds burnout, only balance—a balance of work, rest, play, and prayer.

"There is a time for everything, and a season for every activity under the heavens" (Ecclesiastes 3:1).

▶ **LIE #7: "I am not serving God if I'm not seeing tangible results."**

TRUTH: You are to serve God in the way He chooses, but you are not responsible for God's timing or His harvest.

"So neither the one who plants nor the one who waters is anything, but only God, who makes things grow" (1 Corinthians 3:7).

▶ **LIE #8: "If I don't do everything that I'm asked to do at church, I'm letting God down."**

TRUTH: God is far more interested in having an intimate love relationship with you than He is in what you do.

"Jesus replied, 'Love the Lord your God with all your heart and with all your soul and with all your mind.' This is the first and greatest commandment. And a second is like it: 'Love your neighbor as yourself'" (Matthew 22:37–39).

▶ **LIE #9: "Life is such a burden, I cannot possibly be happy."**

TRUTH: Life is a gift that God wants you to accept with a joyful spirit.

"Moreover, when God gives someone wealth and possessions, and the ability to enjoy them, to accept their lot and be happy in their toil—this is a gift of God" (Ecclesiastes 5:19).

▶ **LIE #10: "I must appear to have it together and not allow my mistakes to show."**

TRUTH: A spirit of humility is more impressive than a spirit of pride.

"For those who exalt themselves will be humbled, and those who humble themselves will be exalted" (Matthew 23:12).

▶ **LIE #11: "Keeping God's laws is the heart of the Christian message."**

TRUTH: Reflecting God's grace is the heart of the Christian message.

"I consider my life worth nothing to me; my only aim is to finish the race and complete the task the Lord Jesus has given me—the task of testifying to the good news of God's grace" (Acts 20:24).

▶ **LIE #12: "When I'm at death's door, I'll be sorry I didn't accomplish more."**

TRUTH: When you're at death's door, your primary regret may be that you didn't show your love more.

"Let no debt remain outstanding, except the continuing debt to love one another, for whoever loves others has fulfilled the law" (Romans 13:8).

HOW TO Replace Stress with Peace

President Abraham Lincoln understood that God had a purpose for his life, and focusing on fulfilling that purpose helped him deal with overwhelming stress.

Lincoln believed the culmination of his lifework was the Emancipation Proclamation, issued on January 1, 1863, during the third year of civil war. Although limited in scope, only calling for the immediate release of slaves in rebel states, it fueled momentum for the Union Army and was a key historical document on the nation's journey to true equality. It also opened the door for black men to join the Union Army and Navy, resulting in more than 200,000 black soldiers and sailors ultimately fighting for the preservation of the nation and freedom for all slaves.[29]

Lincoln later reflected before his faithful friend Joshua Speed concerning that "fatal first of Jany. 41" when he rallied Lincoln and an aspiration for civic greatness was aroused. Concerning the

Emancipation Proclamation, Lincoln told Speed: "I believe in this measure my fondest hopes will be realized."[30] And they were.

But did the esteemed president recognize God had "created" him to do this great work and had even prepared the work for him to do?

> "For we are God's handiwork, created in Christ Jesus to do good works, which God prepared in advance for us to do."
> (Ephesians 2:10)

Tools for Repair

Purpose—Picture God's purpose for you.

Acknowledge that the fast lane is not God's way. Change your thinking to confront a brainwashed world that worships action, activity, and accomplishments. The more you become aware of your identity in Christ, the more you will begin to see the spiritual value of a simple, unpressured lifestyle.

"Yet we urge you, brothers and sisters ... to make it your ambition to lead a quiet life: You should mind your own business and work with your hands, just as we told you, so that your daily life may win the respect of outsiders and so that you will not be dependent on anybody" (1 Thessalonians 4:10–12).

Prayer—Pray specifically for God's provision.

Go to God with every detail of your life. Express your feelings and frustrations honestly. Then acknowledge His faithfulness with an attitude of expectant hope for His provision and thankfulness for His promise to meet all of your needs.

"Do not be anxious about anything, but in every situation, by prayer and petition, with thanksgiving, present your requests to God" (Philippians 4:6).

Protection—Prioritize protection of your time.

Guard your time wisely. Only the enemy speaks to your heart with condemnation and pressure to perform. God's people follow His own example by protecting time in order to rest in Him from overwork and activity.

"There remains, then, a Sabbath-rest for the people of God; for anyone who enters God's rest also rests from their works, just as God did from his" (Hebrews 4:9–10).

Peace—Pray for Christ to give you His peace.

Appropriate the power of Christ to reflect His peace in the way you respond to the pressures and trying circumstances of daily life. This can be a reality if you practice the awareness of His presence, rest completely in Him, and trust totally in His ability to guard your heart from anxiety.

"I have told you these things, so that in me you may have peace. In this world you will have trouble. But take heart! I have overcome the world" (John 16:33).

President Abraham Lincoln was able to reduce stress in his life not only by focusing on what he believed was his divine calling—reuniting a bloodied and devastated country—but also by earnestly and continuously praying.

From the executive mansion on May 9, 1864, Lincoln wrote the following letter to Union supporters: "Enough is known of army operations within the last five days to claim our special gratitude to God. While what remains undone demands our most serious prayers to and reliance upon Him (without whom all human effort is vain), I recommend that all patriots, at their homes, at their places of public worship, and wherever they may be, unite in common thanksgiving and prayer to Almighty God."[31]

Lincoln's rally to pray is similar to Esther's rally to fast to ward off a national tragedy. She directs her cousin Mordecai to *"Go, gather together all the Jews who are in Susa, and fast for me. Do not eat or drink for three days, night or day. I and my attendants will fast as you do"* (Esther 4:15–16).

▶ Stress-reducing prayers[32]

Harvard Medical School researchers used MRIs (magnetic resonance imaging) to identify and characterize the brain regions that are active during a simple form of quiet prayer or meditation. Significant signal increases were observed in the prefrontal cortex, hippocampus, and cingulate cortex of the brain.

- Quiet prayer and meditation activates neural structures involved in attention and control of the autonomic nervous system.
- The Psalms reflect many heartfelt prayers: Psalm 27:7–14; 31:1–5; 51:1–10; single-verse prayers include: Psalm 51:12; 56:3; 63:1.

"Lord, hear my prayer, listen to my cry for mercy; in your faithfulness and righteousness come to my relief" (Psalm 143:1).

▶ **Stress-reducing exercise**

The World Health Organization warns that by the year 2020, depression will be the second leading cause of death and disability in the world, primarily due to more stressful lifestyles, poverty, and violence.[33] Research is conclusive—exercise is one of the best ways to reduce stress.

- Exercise releases the "good" chemicals (for example, dopamine and endorphins) and reduces the "bad" (such as cortisol).[34]
- Make a commitment to exercise (walking, swimming, biking) a minimum of 20 minutes a day, three times a week. Mark your progress on a monthly calendar.

"The wisdom of the prudent is to give thought to their ways, but the folly of fools is deception" (Proverbs 14:8).

▶ Stress-reducing images

Research supports the transforming power of our thoughts—a procedure that is biblical when properly placed. A University of Miami study revealed that focused imagery helped to lower cortisol levels, rates of depression, and levels of mood disturbance and fatigue.[35]

- Visualize green pastures, still waters, and the Lord as your Shepherd—the Lord walking with you during your dark times of deepest stress. Then, repeat very slowly six times: "The Lord is my shepherd ... " Each time emphasize a different word.

"The LORD is my shepherd, I lack nothing. He makes me lie down in green pastures, he leads me beside quiet waters" (Psalm 23:1–2).

▶ Stress-reducing writing

Writing about traumatic experiences can improve psychological and physiological health. Journaling as a part of daily devotions or quiet time helps objectify and analyze stress and traumatic events.

- Take about 20 to 30 minutes a day to pour out your honest and open thoughts and feelings on paper or on the computer.
- Give no thought to grammar, spelling, or punctuation.
- Record your thoughts as they come, not for anyone else's eyes but for your own personal benefit.

"Trust in him at all times, you people; pour out your hearts to him, for God is our refuge" (Psalm 62:8).

▶ Stress-reducing thanksgiving

An "attitude of gratitude" can improve psychological and physiological health. A positive attitude and expectation greatly increase the likelihood of successfully relieving stress and healing trauma wounds. Develop a mind-set of gratefulness and hopefulness by regularly focusing on reasons to be grateful and hopeful.

- Make a list of past "blessings"—answered prayers and acts of kindness by others that lift your spirit, warm your heart, and create within you a sense of goodwill and hopefulness.

- Identify someone each week for whom you are grateful and write a short thank you note or give them a call or text expressing your appreciation for them.

"For everything God created is good, and nothing is to be rejected if it is received with thanksgiving" (1 Timothy 4:4).

▶ Stress-reducing talking

Talking about traumatic experiences can be just as helpful as journaling in improving psychological and physiological health. Verbalizing out loud—to yourself or to another trusted person—the stress-producing events or situations in your life helps identify stressors, objectify and clarify causes, and release negative thoughts and feelings.

- Find someone you trust and consider wise and mature who will agree to be a sounding board for you.

- Meet on a regular basis either weekly or as often as needed and share your stressors, listing each one and exploring the reasons they are stressors in your life.

- Describe your thoughts, feelings, and any traumatic events surrounding them in an open and honest way, not needing to edit your thoughts or weigh your words.

"I am a woman who is deeply troubled. I have not been drinking wine or beer; I was pouring out my soul to the Lord. Do not take your servant for a wicked woman; I have been praying here out of my great anguish and grief" (1 Samuel 1:15–16).

▶ Stress-reducing forgiveness

Releasing resentment and bitterness through extending forgiveness is helpful in improving psychological and physiological health. Letting go of hard feelings and bad attitudes toward others is a great stress reliever and frees the person in bondage to unforgiveness.

- Make a list of those who have hurt or offended you during your lifetime and write beside their names their offenses and the ways you were negatively impacted by them.

- Record your feelings surrounding each event and the pain and stress you have carried as a result.

- Share your list with the Lord and then go back

over it again, this time releasing each person, the offense, and all your pain to Him, trusting Him to deal with the people, their offenses, and your pain as He sees fit.

"Bear with each other and forgive one another if any of you has a grievance against someone. Forgive as the Lord forgave you" (Colossians 3:13).

▶ Stress-reducing touch

Touch significantly reduces stress and improves psychological and physiological health. Therapeutic or compassionate, caring touch or massages expedite emotional healing, slows heart rate, and enhances the autoimmune process.

- Make a conscious effort to touch the people in your life either by giving them a pat on the back, a hug, or a gentle squeeze on the arm or hand.

- Find a good massage therapist and get a massage on a regular basis when stress is bearing down on you.

- Play games with family and friends that involve playful and gentle touch. "Roughhouse" with your children—rolling on the ground together, crawling over each other, or hoisting them onto your shoulders.

"Greet one another with a holy kiss" (2 Corinthians 13:12).

▶ Stress-reducing humor

Humor can serve to improve psychological and physiological health. Using clowns and other laughter-producing methods, especially in children's hospitals, increases the success of medical treatment. Laughter is "good for the soul" and can turn a bad mood into a pleasant one, a tense situation into a relaxed one, and a dark cloud into a silver-lined one.

- Plan fun-filled times on a regular basis with family, friends, and coworkers in an effort to relieve stress or avoid stress buildup.
- Play fun games with loved ones, watch funny movies or sitcoms, read a funny story, share humorous events from your life at least once a month or whenever stress is knocking at your door or the door of someone you care about.

"He will yet fill your mouth with laughter and your lips with shouts of joy" (Job 8:21).

▶ Stress-reducing Scripture

▪ Single verses:

"May these words of my mouth and this meditation of my heart be pleasing in your sight, Lord, my Rock and my Redeemer" (Psalm 19:14).

"The Lord is my light and my salvation—whom shall I fear? The Lord is the stronghold of my life— of whom shall I be afraid?" (Psalm 27:1).

"The Lord is close to the brokenhearted and saves those who are crushed in spirit" (Psalm 34:18).

"Why, my soul, are you downcast? Why so disturbed within me? Put your hope in God, for I will yet praise him, my Savior and my God" (Psalm 42:5).

"My sacrifice, O God, is a broken spirit; a broken and contrite heart you, God, will not despise" (Psalm 51:17).

"The LORD is my strength and my shield; my heart trusts in him, and he helps me. My heart leaps for joy, and with my song I praise him" (Psalm 28:7).

- **Longer passages:**

    "Do not fret because of those who are evil or be envious of those who do wrong ... " (Psalm 37:1–11).

    "I waited patiently for the LORD; he turned to me and heard my cry ... " (Psalm 40:1–8).

    "Hear me, LORD, and answer me, for I am poor and needy ... " (Psalm 86:1–11).

▶ **Stress-reducing meditation**

Meditation is considered the exact opposite of the body's fight-or-flight response under stress.

- Simple meditation can involve sitting in the morning with closed eyes for 10 or 20 minutes. Establish a breathing rhythm, repeating one word (such as *trust* or *forgive*) or a short phrase, over and over.

    ▶ *"I trust in you ..."* (Psalm 25:2).

    ▶ *"The LORD is my strength ... "* (Psalm 28:7).

    ▶ *"You are my hiding place ... "* (Psalm 32:7).

- Repeat in a second session sometime during the day.

▶ Stress-reducing music

Music used today as therapy has historical, biblical precedence. For example, when King Saul was deeply troubled, David played the lyre, or the harp, for him. As a result, 1 Samuel 16:23 says, *"Whenever the spirit from God came on Saul, David would take up his lyre and play. Then relief would come to Saul; he would feel better, and the evil spirit would leave him."* Saul was soothed and refreshed by the beautiful melodies flowing from the strings.

- Listen to classical or praise music.
- Sing inspirational praise music.
- Write meditative spiritual music.
- Put Scripture to music.

"Sing to the LORD with grateful praise; make music to our God on the harp" (Psalm 147:7).

▶ Stress-reducing eating

- Eat at least three meals a day or five small ones. Don't skip or forget meals.
- Avoid fast food, sweets, alcohol, and caffeine. Too much caffeine can have a negative impact on your body when you're under stress. Caffeine impacts the hormones in your body, causing an increase in hormones, such as adrenaline, cortisol, and dopamine.
- Eat healthy food containing
  - ▶ B vitamins: whole grain enriched, fortified products, meat, fish, poultry, oats, fruits
  - ▶ Proteins and iron: meats, eggs, seeds, nuts, etc.

- ▶ A vitamins: green leafy vegetables, sweet potatoes, carrots, eggs, cheddar cheese, etc.
- ▶ C vitamins: citrus fruits, berries, melons, etc.

- Eat food that helps control your sleep and wake cycles—food containing tryptophan (for example, chocolate, oats, cottage cheese, and yogurt). Tryptophan is an *essential* amino acid, which means your body can't produce it, so your diet must supply it. Tryptophan is essential because amino acids are the building blocks of protein. Tryptophan is needed for the body to produce serotonin, which is used to make melatonin, which helps control sleep and wake cycles.

"Then God said, 'I give you every seed-bearing plant on the face of the whole earth and every tree that has fruit with seed in it. They will be yours for food'" (Genesis 1:29).

▶ Stress-reducing pets[36]

If you don't have a furry friend, get one. Owning a dog increases the likelihood of getting out for exercise, which is a known stress buster. Animals offer companionship. They can be the best antidote for loneliness and depression. Pet ownership can help control the spikes in blood pressure brought on by stress and tension.

"Excuse me now," President Abraham Lincoln told an approaching Congressman. "I am going to the theatre. Come and see me in the morning."[37]

Lincoln and his wife, Mary, were devotees of the theater and found it provided a practical way for the war-torn president to stop stress—at least temporarily. On the evening of April 14, 1865, a Good Friday, the Lincolns were in a celebratory mood because the Civil War was officially over and the Confederate Army had surrendered at Appomattox. The pair was attending a production of *Our American Cousin*, but there was a prominent actor present, yet not on stage that evening, who tragically would steal the spotlight.

John Wilkes Booth, enraged that Lincoln declared in a speech that he was planning on giving blacks citizenship and voting rights, eerily vowed, "Now, by God, I'll put him through. That is the last speech he will ever make."[38]

And it was. But God's Word gives this assurance regarding the timing of that fateful evening:

> " ... all the days ordained for me were
> written in your book
> before one of them came to be."
> (Psalm 139:16)

As you seek to slow down your stressful pace, the following suggestions may prove helpful:

▶ **Exercise**—do whatever aerobic activity you enjoy most.

▶ **Take** a few deep breaths—let out a good long sigh.

▶ **Sing** a song at the top of your lungs.

▶ **Practice** muscle relaxation techniques.

▶ **Dim** the lights and take a hot bubble bath while listening to relaxing music.

▶ **Become** better organized—clutter can increase stress.

▶ **Make** your work environment more comfortable.

▶ **Go** for a casual walk in a scenic location.

▶ **Play** a game or paint a picture.

▶ **Invite** friends for a fun-filled evening.

▶ **Have** a good cry once in a while.

▶ **See** a favorite movie or watch a special show.

▶ **Turn** off the television and read an inspiring book.

▶ **Smile** at people and laugh a lot.

▶ **Develop** your faith that God is at work in every situation.

The Bible says ...

> "Come and see what God has done,
> his awesome deeds for mankind!"
> (Psalm 66:5)

Tucked inside the thirteenth chapter of the book of Acts is an obscure passage that is packed with profound wisdom. Acts 13:36 reads, *"Now when David had served God's purpose in his own generation, he fell asleep ... "*

The reference is to King David of Israel, but the implication is both encompassing and enormous. Scripture is telling us that God intentionally places people in the generation that they are in, and when their purpose is finished, *they die.* You and I have been intentionally placed in the generation that we are in, and when our purpose is finished, we will die. And not a day sooner or later than what God has predetermined.

At the close of the Civil War, President Abraham Lincoln no longer was described as stressed and depressed, dark and moody. Two inconceivable words began to be associated with his demeanor— *serene* and *joyful.* Secretary of the Interior, James Harlan, commented that Lincoln seemed "conscious that the great purpose of his life had been achieved. He seemed the very personification of supreme satisfaction."[39]

So when John Wilkes Booth lodged a bullet in the head of the 16th president of the United States of America and killed him, God wasn't taken by surprise. Abraham Lincoln had served God's purpose for his generation, and both God *and Lincoln knew it!*

According to the book of Jeremiah, God's purposes are established even prior to conception. Consider God's words to the prophet:

"Before I formed you in the womb I knew you, before you were born I set you apart; I appointed you as a prophet to the nations." (Jeremiah 1:5)

Your thoughts influence your emotions and your actions. Therefore, it is essential that you take charge of your thinking.

▶ **When the language (thinking) center of your brain is prioritized, the feeling (stress) portion of your brain is reduced.**

Your thoughts dominate and can even dictate your emotions.

▶ **When you are feeling sad, angry, or anxious, check your thoughts.** You will find they correspond to your emotions. Change your thoughts, and you will find your feelings aligning themselves with your thoughts.

Your thoughts are the engine that pulls your emotions like a caboose wherever it goes.

▶ **When your emotions run wild, empower the language center of your brain and you will diminish the power of your feelings.** Activate your thoughts by focusing on the truth.

Your thoughts will eventually bring your feelings into submission to your thinking.

"Do not be anxious about anything, but in every situation, by prayer and petition, with thanksgiving, present your requests to God. And the peace of God, which transcends all understanding, will guard your hearts and your minds in Christ Jesus. Finally, brothers and sisters, whatever is true, whatever is noble, whatever is right, whatever is pure, whatever is lovely, whatever is admirable —if anything is excellent or praiseworthy— think about such things. Whatever you have learned or received or heard from me, or seen in me— put it into practice. And the God of peace will be with you."
(Philippians 4:6–9)

HOW TO Relieve Stress Overload

Toward the end of his life, Abraham Lincoln powerfully modeled for us how to relieve unhealthy stress and how to find a way to bless others in the midst of stressful circumstances.

It begins with a right relationship with God through His Son, Jesus Christ, and an understanding of His sovereignty in all circumstances. There is no better stress reliever than knowing that God is in control of *every* circumstance in our lives.

Next, Lincoln found great relief from unhealthy stress by reading and studying God's Word, the Bible, and by spending time with God in prayer. No doubt, assurances from God's Word about His infinite love, grace, and eagerness to help and rescue fueled Lincoln down the path of greatness.

Lastly, in the midst of stressful circumstances, unhealthy stress was greatly relieved in Lincoln's life through a realization down deep in his soul that his life had purpose. Simply put, Scripture conveys there is no such thing as a *purposeless* life, and that realization alone can be a great stress reducer. Lincoln furthermore understood that he could never fulfill his purpose in his own strength, but through God's strength alone.

Dependence upon Him should dissipate unhealthy stress and provide a powerful dynamic for blessing the lives of others.

One of the most cherished Scriptures addressing stress is found in the book of Philippians.

"Do not be anxious about anything,
but in every situation, by prayer and petition,
with thanksgiving, present your requests to
God. And the peace of God,
which transcends all understanding,
will guard your hearts and
your minds in Christ Jesus."
(Philippians 4:6–7)

Road signs give you notice of impending change or danger. Do you fret when you have to stop for others? Do you resent having to yield the right-of-way? Do you get impatient when necessary repairs call for a reduction in speed and a detour from the familiar? God's warning signs often relay the same messages as the obstacles you encounter on the road.

"Stand at the crossroads and look; ask for the ancient paths, ask where the good way is, and walk in it, and you will find rest for your souls" (Jeremiah 6:16).

Stop

▶ **Stop and look** at the real reason you are experiencing stress.

- Do I try to meet my own needs instead of waiting on the Lord?

- Do I think God cannot get along without me?

- Do I seek self-worth through proving my adequacy and effectiveness?

- Am I Spirit-led or people-pressured?

"Am I now trying to win the approval of human beings, or of God? Or am I trying to please people? If I were still trying to please people, I would not be a servant of Christ" (Galatians 1:10).

▶ **Stop, confess, and turn away** from any known sin in your life.

- Do I manipulate or control others?
- Do I feel envious or jealous of others?
- Do I express my feelings inappropriately?
- Do I overreact to criticism?
- Do I have impure motives?

"Whoever conceals their sins does not prosper, but the one who confesses and renounces them finds mercy" (Proverbs 28:13).

YIELD

▶ **Yield to God's sovereign control** over your circumstances.

- What is God doing in my circumstances?
- In what way does God want me to change?
- How does God want me to respond?
- Do I have impure motives?

"In the LORD's hand the king's heart is a stream of water that he channels toward all who please him" (Proverbs 21:1).

▶ **Yield to God your perceived rights** and your expectations.

- I yield my right to control my circumstances.
- I yield my right to be accepted by others.
- I yield my right to be successful.
- I yield my right to be heard and understood.
- I yield my right to be right.

"Trust in the LORD with all your heart and lean not on your own understanding" (Proverbs 3:5).

RESUME SPEED

▶ **Resume speed**, living in the presence of God.

"Dear Lord,

- I choose to let Christ live His life through me.
- I choose to live in the present, not worrying about tomorrow. I choose to refocus my thoughts from my pressures to Your purposes for allowing this pressure.
- I choose to make a commitment to talk less and listen more.
- I choose to have a thankful heart regardless of the pressure I feel.
- I will call on You, Lord, for wisdom and peace."

"Blessed are those who have learned to acclaim you, who walk in the light of your presence, LORD" (Psalm 89:15).

"Truly my soul finds rest in God; my salvation comes from him." (Psalm 62:1)

SCRIPTURES TO MEMORIZE

What does Jesus say we should do to **find rest for** our **souls**?

*"Come to me, all you who are weary and burdened, and I will give you rest. Take my yoke upon you and learn from me, for I am gentle and humble in heart, and you will **find rest for** your **souls**. For my yoke is easy and my burden is light."* (Matthew 11:28–30)

Why should I strive to achieve **tranquility**?

*"Better one handful with **tranquility** than two handfuls with toil and chasing after the wind."* (Ecclesiastes 4:6)

I feel **hard pressed on every side**. Is it inevitable that I will be **crushed**?

*"We are **hard pressed on every side**, but not **crushed**; perplexed, but not in despair; persecuted, but not abandoned; struck down, but not destroyed."* (2 Corinthians 4:8–9)

Why should I prioritize having **peace** in my **heart**?

*"A **heart** at **peace** gives life to the body ... "* (Proverbs 14:30)

Why should I **cast all** my **anxiety on** Christ?

*"**Cast all** your **anxiety on** him because he cares for you."* (1 Peter 5:7)

Why should I **hope in the Lord**?

*"Those who **hope in the LORD** will renew their strength. They will soar on wings like eagles; they will run and not grow weary, they will walk and not be faint."* (Isaiah 40:31 ESV)

When I was **in distress** and **I cried** out **to God for help**, how can I know if **he heard** me?

*"**In** my **distress** I called to the LORD; **I cried to** my **God for help**. From his temple **he heard** my voice; my cry came before him, into his ears."* (Psalm 18:6)

What **things** are best for me to **think about**—to dwell on?

*" ... whatever is true, whatever is noble, whatever is right, whatever is pure, whatever is lovely, whatever is admirable—if anything is excellent or praiseworthy—**think about** such **things**. ... And the God of peace will be with you."* (Philippians 4:8–9)

How **do** I **not be anxious about anything**?

*"**Do not be anxious about anything**, but in every situation, by prayer and petition, with thanksgiving, present your requests to God. And the peace of God, which transcends all understanding, will guard your hearts and your minds in Christ Jesus."* (Philippians 4:6–7)

NOTES

1. Quoted in Dennis Rainey, *Lonely Husbands, Lonely Wives: Rekindling Intimacy in Every Marriage* (Dallas: Word, 1989), 96.

2. Patricia Cohen, "'Lincoln's Melancholy': Sadder an Wiser" *New York Times*, (New York: NY Times, October 23, 2005), http://www.nytimes.com/2005/10/23/books/review/23cohen.html?pagewanted=all&_r=0.

3. Joshua Wolf Shenk, *Lincoln's Melancholy* (New York: Houghton Mifflin, 2005), 18.

4. Shenk, *Lincoln's Melancholy*, 21.

5. American Psychiatric Association, *Diagnostic and Statistical Manual of Mental Disorders*, 4th ed., text revision (Washington, D.C.: American Psychiatric Association, 2000), 463.

6. *DSM-IV TR*, 463.

7. *DSM-IV TR*, 463.

8. John D. Woodbridge, *More Than Conquerors* (Chicago: Moody, 1992) "Savior of a Nation," 16.

9. Merriam Webster Online Dictionary, s.v. "Distress."

10. W. E. Vine, Merrill F. Unger, and William White, Jr., *Vine's Complete Expository Dictionary of Biblical Words*, electronic ed. (Nashville: Thomas Nelson, 1996), s.v. "Distress."

11. Shenk, *Lincoln's Melancholy*, 43.

12. Shenk, *Lincoln's Melancholy*, 44.

13. Shenk, *Lincoln's Melancholy*, 51.

14. Shenk, *Lincoln's Melancholy*, 95.

15. Shenk, *Lincoln's Melancholy*, 96.

16. Shenk, *Lincoln's Melancholy*, 56.

17. Lloyd John Ogilvie, *Making Stress Work for You: Ten Proven Principles* (Waco, TX: Word, 1985). (Ogilvie divides stress causes under the headings: change, conflict, criticism, concerns, and crises.)

18. Shenk, *Lincoln's Melancholy*, 55.

19. Don Warrick, *How to Handle Stress*, (Colorado Springs, CO: NavPress, 1989), 5–6.

20. Warrick, *How to Handle Stress*, 6.

21. Warrick, *How to Handle Stress*, 6–7.

22. Shenk, *Lincoln's Melancholy*, 65.

23. Benjamin P. Thomas, *Abraham Lincoln: A Biography*, (New York: Knopf, 1952), 195.

24. Carl Sandburg, *The Prairie Years and the War Years*, (New York: Sterling, 2007), 122.

25. Shenk, *Lincoln's Melancholy*, 186.

26. Shenk, *Lincoln's Melancholy*, 193.

27. Sandburg, *The Prairie Years and the War Years*, 122.

28. Sheila Rivera, *The Gettysburg Address*, (Edina, MN: ABDO, 2004), 38.

29. National Archives and Records Administration, "The Emancipation Proclamation" (Washington, DC: NARA, 2008), http://www.archives.gov/exhibits/featured_documents/emancipation_proclamation/.

30. Shenk, *Lincoln's Melancholy*, 190.

31. Abraham Lincoln, *Abraham Lincoln's Pen and Voice* (Cincinnati: R. Clarke and Co., 1890), 360.

32. Herbert Benson and William Proctor, *The Break-Out Principle* (New York: Scribner, 2003), 69–73.

33. World Health Organization, "Depression," http://www.who.int/mental_health/management/depression/definition/en/.

34. Julia Ross, *The Mood Cure* (New York: Penguin, 2004), 32.

35. Cathy H. McKinney, Michael H. Antoni, Mahendra Kumar, Frederick C. Tims, and Philip M. McCabe, "Effects of Guided Imagery and Music (GIM) Therapy on Mood and Cortisol in Healthy Adults," *Health Psychology*, vol. 16(4), ed., Robert Kaplan (Washington, D.C.: American Psychological Association, July 1997), 390–400.

36. Newswise, Pet Dog or Cat Controls Blood Pressure Better than ACE Inhibitor, November 8, 1999, http://www.newswise.com/articles/view/16068/.

37. Shenk, *Lincoln's Melancholy*, 210.

38. Shenk, *Lincoln's Melancholy*, 209.

39. Shenk, *Lincoln's Melancholy*, 208.

HOPE FOR THE HEART TITLES

Adultery .... ISBN 9781596366848
Alcohol & Drug Abuse .... ISBN 9781596366596
Anger .... ISBN 9781596366411
Anorexia & Bulimia .... ISBN 9781596369313
Bullying .... ISBN 9781596369269
Chronic Illness & Disability .... ISBN 9781628621464
Codependency .... ISBN 9781596366510
Conflict Resolution .... ISBN 9781596366473
Confrontation .... ISBN 9781596366886
Considering Marriage .... ISBN 9781596366763
Critical Spirit .... ISBN 9781628621310
Decision Making .... ISBN 9781596366534
Depression .... ISBN 9781596366497
Domestic Violence .... ISBN 9781596366824
Dysfunctional Family .... ISBN 9781596369368
Fear .... ISBN 9781596366701
Financial Freedom .... ISBN 9781596369412
Forgiveness .... ISBN 9781596366435
Friendship .... ISBN 9781596368828
Gambling .... ISBN 9781596366862
Grief .... ISBN 9781596366572
Guilt .... ISBN 9781596366961
Hope .... ISBN 9781596366558
Loneliness .... ISBN 9781596366909
Manipulation .... ISBN 9781596366749
Marriage .... ISBN 9781596368941
Overeating .... ISBN 9781596369467
Parenting .... ISBN 9781596366725
Perfectionism .... ISBN 9781596369214
Procrastination .... ISBN 9781628621648
Reconciliation .... ISBN 9781596368897
Rejection .... ISBN 9781596366787
Self-Worth .... ISBN 9781596366688
Sexual Integrity .... ISBN 9781596366947
Singleness .... ISBN 9781596368774
Spiritual Abuse .... ISBN 9781628621266
Stress .... ISBN 9781596368996
Success Through Failure .... ISBN 9781596366923
Suicide Prevention .... ISBN 9781596366800
Trials .... ISBN 9781628621891
Verbal & Emotional Abuse .... ISBN 9781596366459
Victimization .... ISBN 9781628621365

www.aspirepress.com